W9-AQI-474

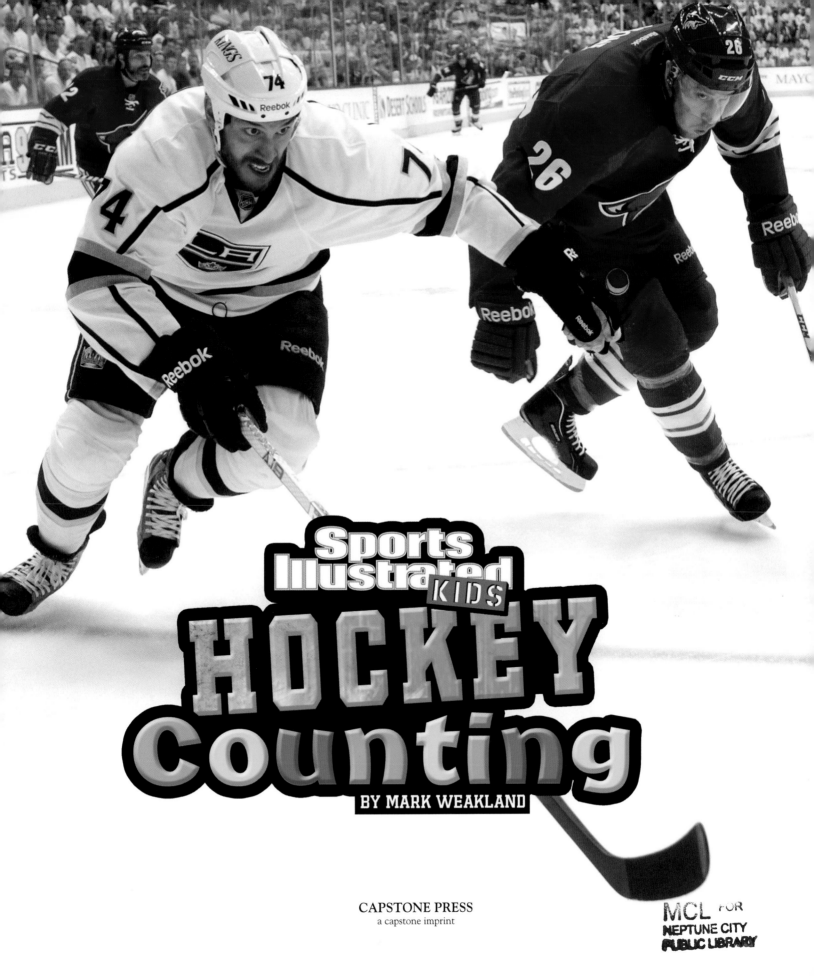

Sports Illustrated KIDS
HOCKEY
Counting

BY MARK WEAKLAND

CAPSTONE PRESS
a capstone imprint

Sports Illustrated Kids Rookie books are published by Capstone Press,
1710 Roe Crest Drive, North Mankato, Minnesota 56003
www.capstonepub.com

Library of Congress Cataloging-in-Publication Data
Weakland, Mark.
 Hockey counting / by Mark Weakland.
  pages cm.—(Sports illustrated kids. SI kids rookie books)
 Includes bibliographical references and index.
 ISBN 978-1-4765-0226-7 (library binding)
 1. Hockey—Juvenile literature. 2. Counting—Juvenile literature. I. Title.
 GV847.25.W42 2014
 796.962—dc23   2013015393

Editorial Credits
Anthony Wacholtz, editor; Ted Williams, designer; Eric Gohl, media researcher;
Eric Manske, production specialist

Photo Credits
Newscom/Icon SMI: Chris Williams, 22–23, Rich Kane, 20–21; Shutterstock: BrunoRosa,
18–19, Vladislav Gajic, 26–27; *Sports Illustrated:* Damian Strohmeyer, 8–9, David E. Klutho, 1,
4–5, 6–7, 10–11, 12–13, 14–15, 16–17, 24–25, Robert Beck, cover, 3, 28–29

Printed in the United States of America in North Mankato, Minnesota.
032013   007223CGF13

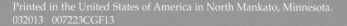

Sticks in hand, hockey players leap onto the ice. They've been counting the minutes until they can get in the game. **Let's play hockey and start counting too!**

1

There's just **one** Stanley Cup trophy, and only the best team wins it each year. One happy player hoists the Cup as the crowd cheers.

2

When do hockey players look exactly the same? When they are twins! The **two** brothers skate side-by-side in every game.

Hockey is played all over the world. In the Olympics, teams from many countries compete for medals. **Three** Canadian athletes proudly show their Olympic gold medals.

3

Goalies use all **four** limbs—two arms and two legs—to keep the puck out of the net. With his limbs spread wide, the goalie looks like a big X on the ice.

5

Hockey is a team sport. Players work together to win games. **Five** skaters celebrate after scoring a goal.

Each hockey team is allowed **six** players on the ice at a time. Five skaters and one goalie wait patiently for the game to begin.

Seven players have their eyes on the puck. Surrounded by players in blue, two forwards scramble as they try to score.

8

A row of **eight** stick blades rests on the ice. Soon the same blades will slap the puck and send it flying.

Nine players line up to shake hands. It's a tradition for hockey players to shake hands at the end of a game. Handshakes are a sign of good sportsmanship.

With muscles tensed, opposing teams wait for the puck to drop. The moment the puck hits the ice, **ten** crouching skaters explode into action.

Eleven players crowd near the goal. Six players look on as their five opponents celebrate. Their team has just scored!

Far from the action, an equipment shelf holds **twelve** hockey helmets. The helmets and other equipment protect players from flying pucks and swinging sticks.

One puck, two skates, three goals for a hat trick. Hockey has many things to count.

Olympic skaters stretch before the game. How many hockey players do you see? Start counting!

Glossary

forward—a hockey player whose main job is to move the puck toward the opponent's net and try to score goals

hat trick—when a player scores three goals in one game

hoist—raise

limb—a part of the body used in moving or grasping; arms and legs are limbs

Olympics—a competition of many sports events held every four years in a different country; people from around the world compete against one another

opposing—on opposite teams

sportsmanship—playing a sport or game respectfully and fairly

tradition—a custom, idea, or belief passed down through time

Read More

Frederick, Shane. *The Best of Everything Hockey Book.* Sports Illustrated Kids. North Mankato, Minn.: Capstone Press, 2011.

Jordan, Christopher. *Hockey 123.* Plattsburgh, N.Y.: Fenn/Tundra, 2011.

Shea, Kevin. *H Is for Hockey: An NHL Alumni Alphabet.* Ann Arbor, Mich.: Sleeping Bear Press, 2012.

Internet Sites

FactHound offers a safe, fun way to find Internet sites related to this book. All of the sites on FactHound have been researched by our staff.

Here's all you do:

Visit *www.facthound.com*

Type in this code: 9781476502267

Check out projects, games and lots more at
www.capstonekids.com

Index